What

Russ De Somer
Photos by Brooke Dunkley

What Knot To Wear

Copyright © 2012 by Russ De Somer

All rights reserved. No part of this publication may be reproduced, stored in a retrieval system, or transmitted by any means—electronic, mechanical, photographic (photocopying), recording or otherwise—without prior permission in writing from the author.

Printed in the United States of America

ISBN 13: 978-1461135081

Photographs by Brooke Dunkley

Models, William Cosman and Russ De Somer.

For more information please visit: www.whatknot2wear.com

Acknowledgments

First I would like to thank my Father in Heaven for all He has given me in this life. Additionally, I want like to thank my beautiful wife Alena and my kids for all their support during this project. I would also like to thank Richard Paul Evans for inspiring me to take a risk and write a book. It was Rick who taught me that in order to be successful, you have to take risks. I am grateful for Blair Williams, a fellow tie connoisseur, who gave me the idea for this book. To all my Book Wise friends whose passion for books helped motivate me to finish. I thank you all!

A special thank you to Josh Petersen who was the original artist for the book. I ultimately decided to go in a different direction with the book but you are an amazing artist.

Thanks to my brother and sister-in-law, William and Gretel Cosman. William, thanks for your patience with posing for two photo shoots. And Gretel, thank you for lending me William and also for editing the book. I couldn't have done it without you.

Finally, thanks to my photographer Brooke Dunkley. You did a great job. Make sure to go to my website for a link to Brooke's web page.

Contents

Why I wrote this book ✦ 7

A Brief History of the Necktie ✦ 11

How to Tie a Necktie ✦ 15

The Four In Hand ✦ 19

The Windsor ✦ 29

The Half Windsor ✦ 43

The Pratt/Shelby ✦ 55

The Plattsburgh ✦ 65

The St. Andrew ✦ 77

The Cavendish ✦ 89

The Nicky Knot ✦ 103

The Oriental ✦ 113

The Classic Bow Tie ✦ 121

Proper Necktie Care ✦ 135

What Knot To Wear

Why I Wrote This Book

What Knot To Wear

In the book, "*5 Lesson a Millionaire Taught Me About Life and Wealth*" Richard Paul Evans talks about Winning in the Margins and Giving Back. Winning in the margins simply means, finding ways to make extra money to apply to one's nest egg. Initially, this was my goal for writing *What Knot to Wear*. I thought I could make enough money to get out of debt and start saving a little more for retirement. As I talked to people about my book, I realized that I might just have something that could not only bless my life, but could bless the lives of others as well. Giving back, as Richard Paul Evans calls it, is showing gratitude for what you have by sharing it with others. For this reason, a portion of every book I sell on my website, **www.whatknot2wear.com**, will go to the Christmas Box International.

The Christmas Box International partners with local and international communities and groups to prevent child abuse and to improve the quality of life for children who have been abused

Why I Wrote This Book

or neglected. The Christmas Box International also helps children through the Life Start Initiative. Each year over 24,000 youths age out of the foster care system in America. These are teens that were never adopted or able to return to the homes from which they were removed due to abuse, neglect and/or abandonment. Many of these individuals leave foster care as young as 18 years old. They face almost insurmountable challenges as they try to navigate the difficulties of adulthood, including incarceration, substance abuse, teen pregnancy, mental illness, poverty, homelessness and suicide. With no one to help them, many of them return to abusive situations or end up homeless on the streets.

The Christmas Box International has come up with a four phase plan to involve the community in helping these youths. Through this book, I hope to accomplish both tasks; to Win In the Margins and to Give Back.

I truly hope you enjoy this book! I had a lot of fun putting it together.

What Knot To Wear

A Brief History
of the
Necktie

What Knot To Wear

Much debate exists as to the first historical references to the necktie. Buried in 210 BC, the first emperor of China, Shin Huang Ti, had 7500 life-size terra cotta replicas of his army made to guard him in the after world. They all wore neck scarves which could be construed as the first necktie in history.

The first recognized neckties were noted around 1635, when roughly 6000 knights, and soldiers visited Paris to show their allegiance to King Louis XIV and Cardinal Richelieu. The Croatian mercenaries in the group wore uniforms that utilized cloth scarves tied around their necks. The ties were of various fabrics depending on the ranks of the soldiers: course cloth for a common soldier and perhaps silk for an officer. The French were quite taken with the new "Croatian style"

In 1650, Louis XIV officially recognized this fashion trend. It was most notably implemented in the courts where military style was much admired. This gave rise to a new term, "a la croate" which eventually turned into the French word for necktie, "la cravate"

When Charles II returned from exile in 1660, he brought with him the latest fashion craze, the cravat. Over the next several years, the cravat spread across Europe and into the American colonies to the point that no dignified man would be caught dead without something tied around his neck. These could have been strings with tassels, lace, silk, ribbon, *ad infinitum*. The sky was the limit. At one point there were over 100 recognized ways to tie a cravat.

A Brief History of the Necktie

The early 1700's brought about the Steinkirk, a scarf that was loosely wrapped around the neck with the end tucked into or pinned to the shirt. Even the women got in on this trend, the only notable difference being that the women's Steinkirk's were vividly colored while the men wore plain white.

Life on the plantations of the south in the 1800's was much too hot to wear anything around the neck. As necessity is the mother of invention, distinguished gentlemen fashioned bowties out of ribbon. This was much thinner and cooler than the traditional scarf.

Jean Patou, a fashion designer in the 1920's, developed the "designer" necktie. He made them out of the fabric left over from the women's fashions. We can thank Monsieur Patou for what today's businessmen wear around the neck. Today's neckties have come a long way from the silk scarves worn around the terra cotta soldiers in Emperor Shin Huang Ti's tomb almost 2200 years ago.

What Knot To Wear

How to Tie a Necktie

What Knot To Wear

You may ask yourself, "Self, why do I need to know more than one knot for my tie?" The answer is really quite simple. Different ties with their varying thicknesses and widths look better with different knots. This does not even take into consideration the collar style of your shirt. For example, if you wear a shirt with a wide spread collar, a Windsor looks perfect, while a Four In Hand knot looks much too diminutive. By the same token, if you wear a shirt with a long slender collar, a smaller knot such as a Pratt or a Half Windsor works nicely and does not make you look like you have a grapefruit under your chin. I recommend that you take several of your favorite ties and try the different knots on each one. Pay attention to the way the knot sits in the collar. I like to write the type of knot I use with a particular tie on the label on the back.

In this book, we are going to explore nine knots plus the classic bow tie. While there are many knots to choose from, four in particular are used most often. The most commonly used knot is the Four In Hand. Probably 80% of all people who wear a tie use this knot. It the easiest to learn and most frequently taught of all the knots. The next three knots are used less frequently, but have a more classic look and feel. They are the Windsor, the Half Windsor and the Pratt. Most of my personal ties are relatively thick so I use the Half Windsor and the Pratt the majority of the time. I also have a long torso so it is important for me to have as much of the wide part of the tie available. For this reason, the Windsor does not work well for me as too much

How to Tie a Necktie

of the tie is tied up in the knot. (Pardon the pun!)

The illustrations in this book are shown to you as if you are looking into the mirror. You will always be working with the fat part of the tie. Remember this while reading the descriptions. With the exception of the first couple of steps where it is important to note which part of the tie is being referenced, the working part or fat part of the tie will be referenced as simply "The Tie".

There are two types of knots: those that are self-releasing and those that are true knots. You can tell which knots will release themselves by how you start the tie. Any knot that starts with the front of the tie facing outward is a self-releasing knot. All the knots that start with the back facing outward are essentially just tied around the narrow end of the tie. Extra caution should be taken when untying a knot that does not release itself. These can cinch very tight and damage the tie.

This book is not designed to tell you which knot is the perfect knot for you but simply to give you more options when tying your ties to get just the right look for the occasion. Experimentation and personal taste are the keys to finding the right knot for you. So grab some ties and let's figure out "What Knot to Wear!"

What Knot To Wear

The Four In Hand

The knot known as the "Four In hand" is arguably the most well known and commonly worn knot today. Most likely over 80% of people who wear ties use this knot.

The name of this knot is derived from the Four In Hand carriage in the mid-1800's. The name has reference to the way the drivers tied the reigns of their carriage with this knot. The Four in hand is a small knot with a distinctive elongated, asymmetric shape.

What Knot To Wear

Step 1

To start the Four In Hand, the tie should be positioned on the neck so that the wide part of the tie is on the right and the narrow side is on the left. The front of the tie should be facing outward.

The Four In Hand

Step 2

Take the fat side and cross it over the top of the narrow side.

What Knot To Wear

Step 3

Wrap the tie around the back from left to right.

The Four In Hand

Step 4

Wrap the tie around the front from right to left.

What Knot To Wear

Step 5

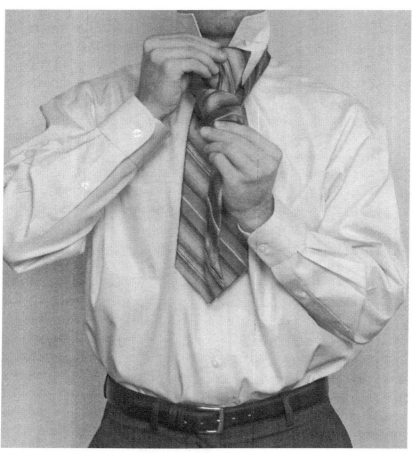

Pull the tie up through the neck opening from the back.

The Four In Hand

Step 6

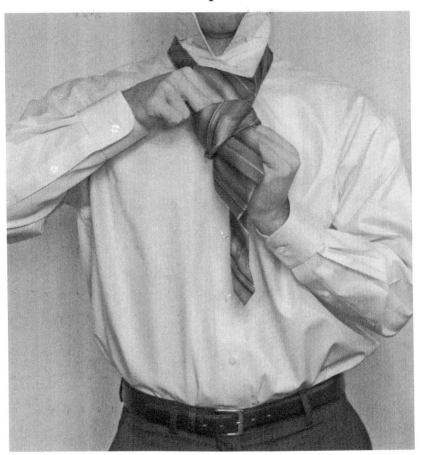

Push the tie through the loop created by wrapping the tie around the front.

Step 7

Pull the fat end of the tie downwards and cinch it tight. Make any adjustments necessary to the knot.

The Four In Hand

Step 8

The finished knot should be a slender asymmetrical knot like you see here.

What Knot To Wear
The Windsor

The Windsor knot, also known as the Double-Windsor or Full Windsor, is probably as well known as the Four In Hand.

The Windsor is a large, symmetrical, triangular-shaped knot. Somewhere between the 1920's through the 1930's, Americans named this knot after the Duke of Windsor who was known for his liking of excessively large triangular-shaped knots on his ties. He achieved this look, partially with the knot and additionally with custom made extra thick ties.

What Knot To Wear

Step 1

To start the Windsor, the tie should be positioned on the neck so that the wide part of the tie is on the right and the narrow side is on the left. The front of the tie should be facing outward.

The Windsor

Step 2

Take the fat side and cross it over the top of the narrow side.

What Knot To Wear

Step 3

Pull the tie up through the neck opening from the back.

The Windsor

Step 4

Pull the tie down and to the left.

What Knot To Wear

Step 5

Wrap the tie around the back to the right.

The Windsor

Step 6

Push the tie down through the neck opening from the front.

Step 7

Pull the tie down and to the right.

The Windsor

Step 8

Wrap the tie around the front from right to left.

Step 9

Pull the tie through the neck opening from the back.

The Windsor

Step 10

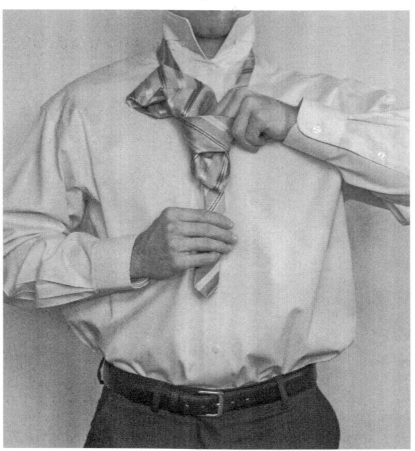

Push the tie through the loop created by wrapping the tie around the front.

Step 11

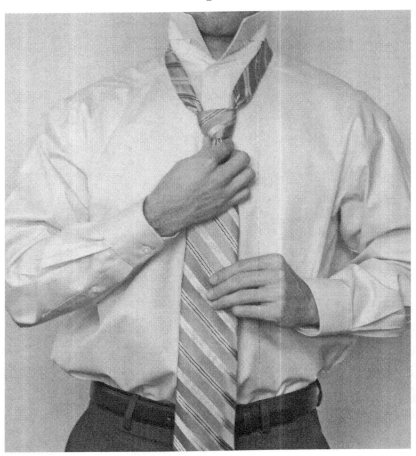

Pull the fat end of the tie downwards and cinch it tight. Make any adjustments necessary to the knot.

The Windsor

Step 12

The final knot should be a symmetrical large knot. The size of the knot will depend greatly on the thickness of the tie.

What Knot To Wear
The Half Windsor

The Half Windsor is almost as well known as the Windsor. This knot is a medium-sized symmetrical triangle that can be worn with most collar sizes and spreads

The Half Windsor is not truly half of a Windsor; it is closer to three-quarters.

What Knot To Wear

Step 1

To start the Half Windsor, the tie should be positioned on the neck so that the wide part of the tie is on the right and the narrow side is on the left. The front of the tie should be facing outward.

The Half Windsor

Step 2

Take the fat side and cross it over the top of the narrow side.

What Knot To Wear

Step 3

Wrap the tie around the back from left to right.

The Half Windsor

Step 4

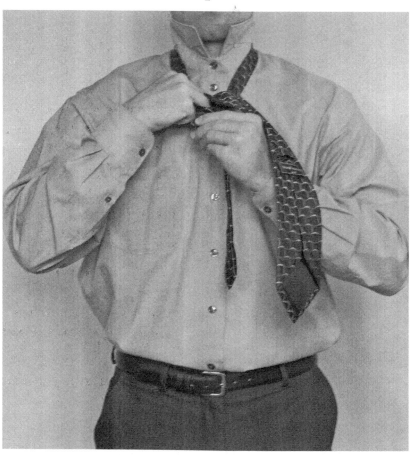

Push the tie through the neck opening from the front.

What Knot To Wear

Step 5

Pull the tie down and to the right. This will make the right side of the tie larger than the left.

The Half Windsor

Step 6

Wrap the tie around the front from right to left.

What Knot To Wear

Step 7

Push the tie through the neck opening in the back.

The Half Windsor

Step 8

Push the tie through the loop created by wrapping the tie around the front.

Step 9

Pull the fat end of the tie downwards and cinch it tight. Make any adjustments necessary to the knot.

The Half Windsor

Step 10

The final knot should be a symmetrical medium-sized knot.

What Knot To Wear
The Pratt/Shelby

The Pratt or Shelby knot is a compact, medium-sized symmetrical knot. The Pratt is comparable in size to a Half Windsor however it is not self releasing and must be untied when the tie is removed.

The Pratt is one of several knots that starts in an inverted position with the underside of the knot facing outward. This in effect saves one loop.

What Knot To Wear

Step 1

To start the Pratt/Shelby, the tie should be positioned on the neck so that the wide part of the tie is on the right and the narrow side is on the left. The back of the tie should be facing outward.

The Pratt/Shelby

Step 2

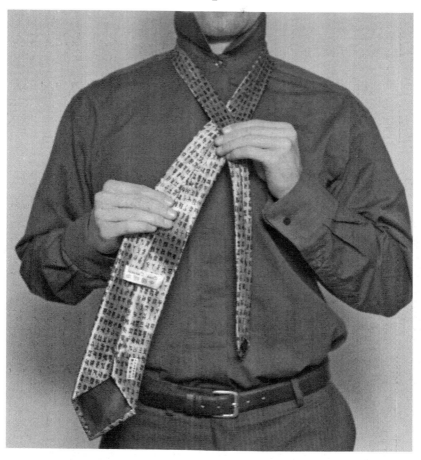

Take the fat side and cross it under the narrow side.

What Knot To Wear

Step 3

Push the tie through the neck opening from the front.

The Pratt/Shelby

Step 4

Pull the tie down and to the left.

Step 5

Wrap the tie around the front from left to right.

The Pratt/Shelby

Step 6

Pull the tie up through the neck opening from the back.

What Knot To Wear

Step 7

Push the tie through the loop created by wrapping the tie around the front.

The Pratt/Shelby

Step 8

Pull the fat end of the tie downwards and cinch it tight. Make any adjustments necessary to the knot.

What Knot To Wear

Step 9

The finished knot will be an elongated symmetrical knot. This knot works well for pointed collars.

What Knot To Wear
The Plattsburgh

The Plattsburgh knot is named for the town in up-state New York where the creator of this knot, Thomas Fink, was born. The Plattsburgh has a distinct shape of a very wide symmetrical triangle with a small opening at the bottom.

What Knot To Wear

Step 1

To start the Plattsburgh, the tie should be positioned on the neck so that the wide part of the tie is on the right and the narrow side is on the left. The back of the tie should be facing outward.

The Plattsburgh

Step 2

Take the fat side and cross it under the narrow side.

What Knot To Wear

Step 3

Pinch the tie in the middle and lift up the fat part of the tie.

The Plattsburgh

Step 4

Push the tie through the neck opening from the front.

What Knot To Wear

Step 5

Pull the tie down and to the right.

The Plattsburgh

Step 6

Push the tie through the neck opening from the front.

What Knot To Wear

Step 7

Pull the tie down and to the left.

The Plattsburgh

Step 8

Wrap the tie around the front from left to right.

What Knot To Wear

Step 9

Push the tie through the loop created by wrapping the tie around the front.

The Plattsburgh

Step 10

Pull the fat end of the tie downwards and cinch it tight. Make any adjustments necessary to the knot.

What Knot To Wear

Step 11

The finished knot will be a medium-sized symmetrical knot.

What Knot To Wear
The St. Andrew

The St. Andrew is a close cousin to the Plattsburgh. In size, it falls somewhere between the Windsor and Half Windsor knots but is more narrow than both. Although this knot starts with the back facing outward, it is a self-releasing knot.

What Knot To Wear

Step 1

To start the St. Andrew, the tie should be positioned on the neck so that the wide part of the tie is on the right and the narrow side is on the left. The back of the tie should be facing outward.

The St. Andrew

Step 2

Take the fat side and cross it under the narrow side.

Step 3

Wrap the tie around the front from left to right.

The St. Andrew

Step 4

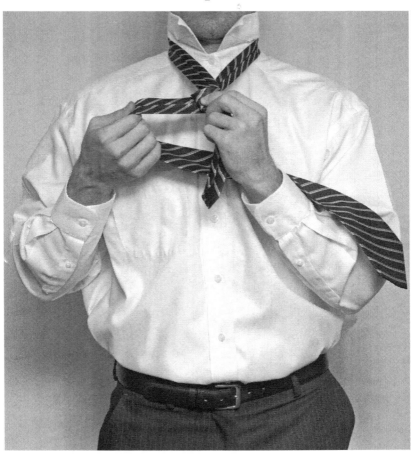

Wrap the tie around the back from right to left.

Step 5

Push the tie through the neck opening from the front.

The St. Andrew

Step 6

Pull the tie down and to the right.

What Knot To Wear

Step 7

Wrap the tie around the front from right to left.

The St. Andrew

Step 8

Pull the tie up through the neck opening from the back.

What Knot To Wear

Step 9

Push the tie through the loop created by wrapping the tie around the front.

The St. Andrew

Step 10

Pull the fat end of the tie downwards and cinch it tight. Make any adjustments necessary to the knot.

What Knot To Wear

Step 11

The finished knot will be a medium to large short knot with a symmetrical shape.

What Knot To Wear
The Cavendish

The Cavendish is another knot by Thomas Fink. He designed this knot with his co-author, fellow university physicist Yong Mao. They named the knot after the Cavendish Laboratories where the two worked and co-wrote the book *"85 Ways To Tie a Tie."*

The knot is basically two Four In Hand knots mirroring each other, giving it a similar shape but considerably larger in size.

What Knot To Wear

Step 1

To start the Cavendish, the tie should be positioned on the neck so that the wide part of the tie is on the right and the narrow side is on the left. The front of the tie should be facing outward.

The Cavendish

Step 2

Take the fat side and cross it over the top of the narrow side.

What Knot To Wear

Step 3

Wrap the tie around the back from left to right.

The Cavendish

Step 4

Wrap the tie around the front from right to left.

What Knot To Wear

Step 5

Pull the tie up through the neck opening from the back.

The Cavendish

Step 6

Pull the tie down and to the right.

What Knot To Wear

Step 7

Wrap the tie around the back from right to left.

The Cavendish

Step 8

Wrap the tie around the front from left to right.

What Knot To Wear

Step 9

Pull the tie up through the neck opening from the back.

The Cavendish

Step 10

Push the tie through the loop created by wrapping the tie around the front.

What Knot To Wear

Step 11

Pull the fat end of the tie downwards and cinch it tight. Make any adjustments necessary to the knot.

The Cavendish

Step 12

The finished knot will be a large wide symmetrical knot.

What Knot To Wear
The Nicky Knot

The Nicky is related to the Pratt and also gives a symmetrical medium-sized knot. The Nicky is very versatile and can be used with just about any tie.

Like its cousin the Pratt, it starts out with the back facing outward.

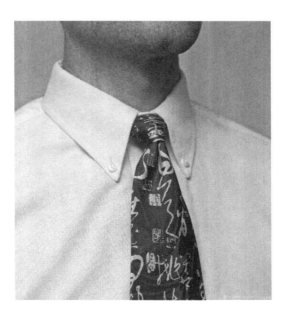

What Knot To Wear

Step 1

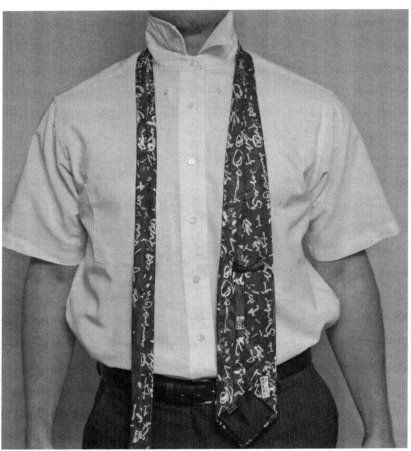

To start the Nicky, the tie should be positioned on the neck so that the wide part of the tie is on the right and the narrow side is on the left. The back of the tie should be facing outward.

The Nicky Knot

Step 2

Take the fat side and cross it under the narrow side.

What Knot To Wear

Step 3

Push the tie through the neck opening from the front.

The Nicky Knot

Step 4

Pull the tie down and to the right.

What Knot To Wear

Step 5

Wrap the tie around the front from right to left.

The Nicky Knot

Step 6

Pull the tie up through the neck opening from the back.

What Knot To Wear

Step 7

Push the tie through the loop created by wrapping the tie around the front.

The Nicky Knot

Step 8

Pull the fat end of the tie downwards and cinch it tight. Make any adjustments necessary to the knot.

Step 9

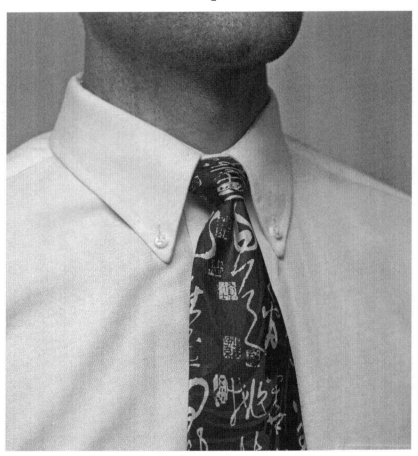

The finished knot will be a small slightly elongated knot that is symmetrical in shape.

What Knot To Wear
The Oriental Knot

The Oriental knot is very efficient and uses as few movements as possible. It is a very simple knot and is quite popular among young Chinese people, thus the name.

This knot also starts with the back facing outward (like the Pratt and the Nicky) and is particularly well-suited to both heavy wool and thick silk ties that would be much too bulky with another knot. You could almost consider this a reverse Four In Hand.

What Knot To Wear

Step 1

To start the Oriental, the tie should be positioned on the neck so that the wide part of the tie is on the right and the narrow side is on the left. The back of the tie should be facing outward.

The Oriental Knot

Step 2

Take the fat side and cross it under the narrow side.

What Knot To Wear

Step 3

Wrap the tie around the front from left to right.

The Oriental Knot

Step 4

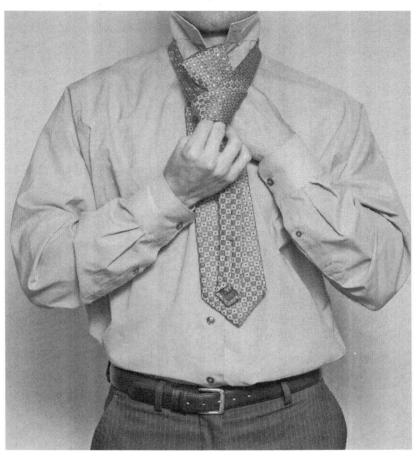

Pull the tie up though the neck opening from the back.

What Knot To Wear

Step 5

Push the tie through the loop created by wrapping the tie around the front.

The Oriental Knot

Step 6

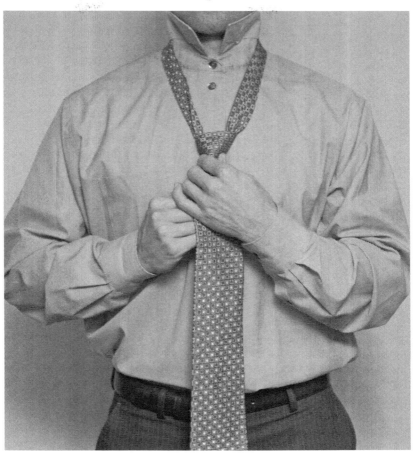

Pull the fat end of the tie downwards and cinch it tight. Make any adjustments necessary to the knot.

What Knot To Wear

Step 7

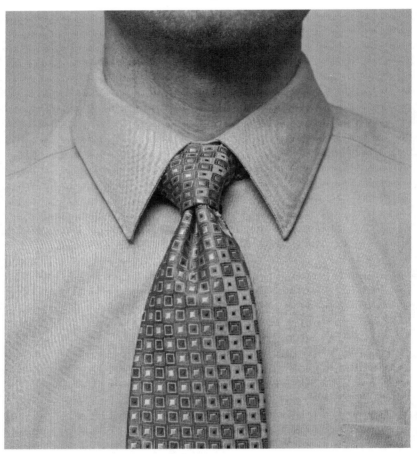

The finished knot will be very small and asymmetrical when using a thin tie. Our model here used a very thick tie, resulting in a large asymmetrical knot.

What Knot To Wear
The Classic Bow Tie

The Bow Tie has somewhat of a Jekyll and Hyde reputation. On one hand, it can be part of the stereotypical wardrobe of someone considered to be a "nerd" such as a scientist or a librarian.

On the other hand, bow ties are the epitome of sophistication. What would a "black tie" affair be without the classic bow tie? A tuxedo can certainly be worn with some other type of neck scarf such as an ascot, but when we think of a tux and tails, the first thing that pops into our minds is that all-important bow tie.

The key to a classy looking bow tie, ironically, is slight imperfection. If it is too perfect, it looks like a pre-tied prom tie (not that there is anything wrong with those).

What Knot To Wear

Step 1

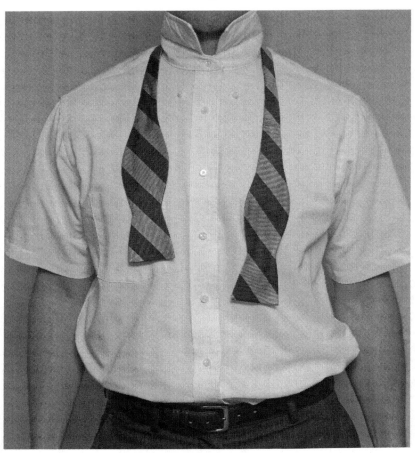

The Bow Tie will start with the right side hanging down lower than the left.

The Classic Bow Tie

Step 2

Take the right side and cross it over the top of the left side.

What Knot To Wear

Step 3

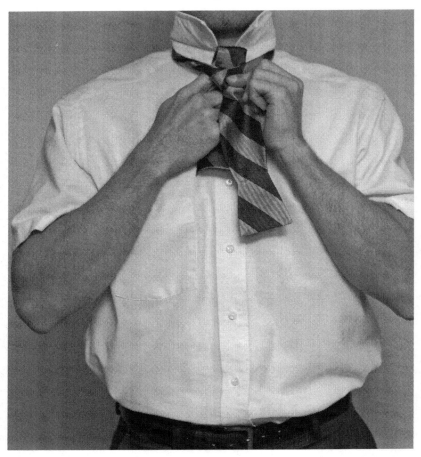

Pull the left side up though the neck opening from the back.

The Classic Bow Tie

Step 4

This essentially forms an overhand knot. Cinch it somewhat tight.

What Knot To Wear

Step 5

Take the right side and fold it in half. Pinch and hold the knot in the center.

The Classic Bow Tie

Step 6

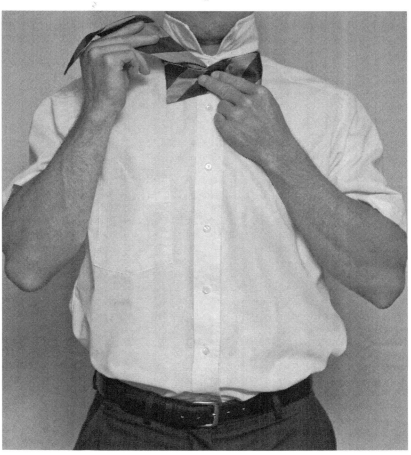

Take the left side and wrap it up and over the folded part you just created.

What Knot To Wear

Step 7

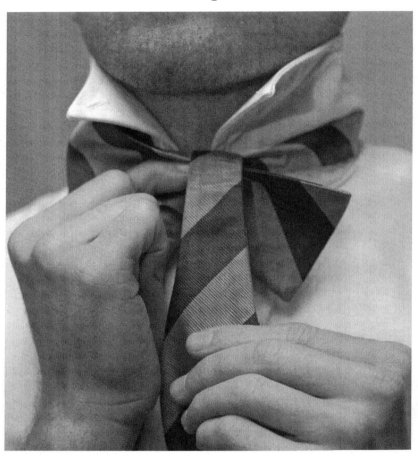

Pull the end of the tie down over the folded end.

The Classic Bow Tie

Step 8

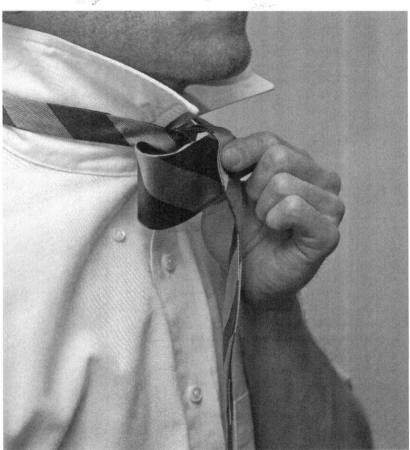

Pinch the end you just pulled down along with the folded tie and pull it out slightly. This will create an opening. Be careful not to grab the overhand knot section next to the collar.

What Knot To Wear

Step 9

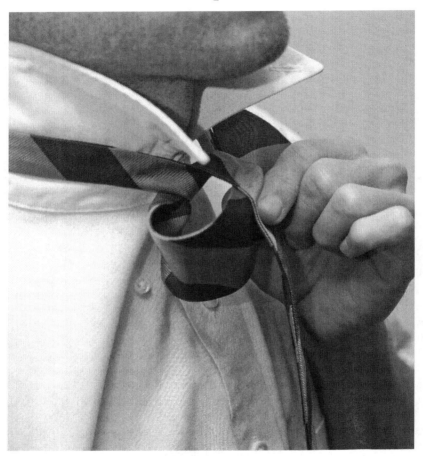

This picture illustrates the loop created from another angle.

The Classic Bow Tie

Step 10

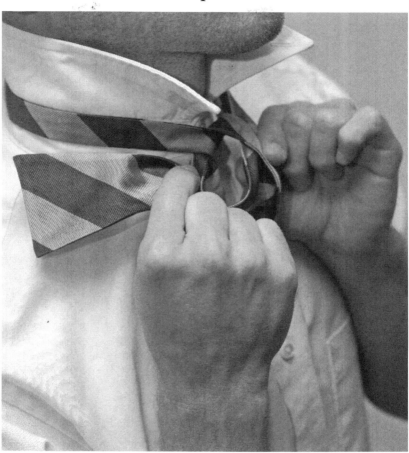

Take the end that is hanging down and grab it in the middle. Push it through the opening you have created in the tie.

What Knot To Wear

Step 11

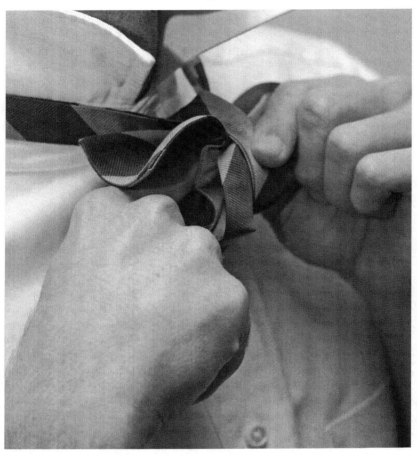

Use your finger to push it all the way through.

The Classic Bow Tie

Step 12

Pull the ends tight and adjust until both sides are even. The final knot will look like this.

What Knot To Wear

Proper Necktie Care

What Knot To Wear

Hanging up your neckties on a coat hanger or rolling them up are the preferred methods of tie storage.

Rolling your tie up starting with the narrow end and letting it be for a few days will remove most of the wrinkles in a tie. Another quicker alternative is to hang your tie up in the bathroom while you take a hot shower, the steam will help with the wrinkles.

Storing ties in direct sunlight will cause them to fade. They should be in a closet or drawer where they can be protected.

When traveling, ties can be carefully folded and placed in your suit coat pocket or loosely rolled up and placed inside a pair of socks.

NEVER pull loose threads on your tie. Cut them with scissors or nail clippers.

NEVER leave your tie in the knot after you remove it. It may seem convenient when you get your tie exactly the correct length but it will damage your tie and cause permanent wrinkles.

NEVER pull your tie off. To untie it, simply reverse the directions you used to tie it.

If you absolutely must iron your tie, be sure to cover it with a cloth and set your iron to the lowest setting.

Be careful not to get anything on your tie. Washing it with

Proper Necktie Care

water will damage the tie and cause the fabric to shrink unevenly.

You should never take your tie to the dry cleaners. When they press it, the shine and luster of the tie will become dulled.

When in doubt, read the care label on your tie.

Made in the USA
Lexington, KY
23 December 2015